ABOUT THIS BOOK

{ SUGAR SKULLS }

AN ADULT COLORING BOOK

"Whether you would consider yourself artistic or not, research points to the importance of incorporating a little bit of creativity in our daily lives."

Unless you've been living under a rock, you've no doubt heard that coloring is making a huge comeback in the adult world. No longer are crayons and colored pencils solely the instrument of the elementary school artist — professionals and parents from all walks of life are realizing the benefits of sitting down with a good old fashioned coloring book. But coloring is more than just a hobby or way to spend a Sunday afternoon, it can actually benefit your life in a variety of ways.

According to a January 2016 article by CNN, "Coloring books are no longer just for the kids. In fact, adult coloring books are all the rage right now. And while researchers and art therapists alike have touted the calming benefits for over a decade, it's childhood favorite Crayola that's gotten adult coloring books some serious grown-up attention. The famous crayon makers just launched a set of markers, colored pencils and a collection of adult coloring books, Coloring Escapes, last month.

And though the first commercially successful adult coloring books were published in 2012 and 2013, the once-niche hobby has now grown into a full-on trend, with everyone from researchers at Johns Hopkins University to the editors of Yoga Journal suggesting coloring as an alternative to meditation."

We hope you enjoy this coloring book!

www.HappyCreekDesigns.com

www.HappyCreekDesigns.com

www.HappyCreekDesigns.com

www.HappyCreekDesigns.com

www.HappyCreekDesigns.com

www.HappyCreekDesigns.com

www.HappyCreekDesigns.com

www.HappyCreekDesigns.com

www.HappyCreekDesigns.com

www.HappyCreekDesigns.com

www.HappyCreekDesigns.com

www.HappyCreekDesigns.com

www.HappyCreekDesigns.com

www.HappyCreekDesigns.com

www.HappyCreekDesigns.com

www.HappyCreekDesigns.com

www.HappyCreekDesigns.com

www.HappyCreekDesigns.com

www.HappyCreekDesigns.com

www.HappyCreekDesigns.com

www.HappyCreekDesigns.com

www.HappyCreekDesigns.com

www.HappyCreekDesigns.com

www.HappyCreekDesigns.com

www.HappyCreekDesigns.com

www.HappyCreekDesigns.com

www.HappyCreekDesigns.com

www.HappyCreekDesigns.com

www.HappyCreekDesigns.com

www.HappyCreekDesigns.com

www.HappyCreekDesigns.com

www.HappyCreekDesigns.com

www.HappyCreekDesigns.com

www.HappyCreekDesigns.com

www.HappyCreekDesigns.com

www.HappyCreekDesigns.com

www.HappyCreekDesigns.com

www.HappyCreekDesigns.com

Made in the USA
Middletown, DE
30 April 2024

53679626R00044